This publication has been
made possible
by a grant from the
National Endowment for the Humanities
Washington, D. C.

The Chinese Exhibition

A pictorial record of the
Exhibition of Archaeological Finds
of The People's Republic of China

National Gallery of Art
Washington, D.C.
December 13, 1974-March 30, 1975

The Nelson Gallery-Atkins Museum
Kansas City, Missouri
April 20-June 8, 1975

Asian Art Museum of San Francisco
The Avery Brundage Collection
San Francisco, California
June 28-August 28, 1975

SAN FRANCISCO SPONSORS

National Endowment for the Humanities

Asian Art Commission
The San Francisco Foundation
IBM Corporation
Bank of America Foundation
Standard Oil Company of California
The Chinese-American Committee
Asian Art Foundation of San Francisco

TITLE PAGE
Calligraphy by Kuo Mo-jo
Vice-Chairman of the Standing Committee of the
National People's Congress of The People's
Republic of China
President of the Academy of Sciences of China.

The Committee for the Organization of Exhibitions of
Archaeological Finds of The People's Republic of
China has supplied the majority of photographs and
other graphic material appearing in this publication.

Robert Harding Associates, Ltd., London and
The Times Newspaper Ltd., London, have supplied
the remainder.

Cover Photo: Per-Olle Stackman, Stockholm

COVER
218 Bronze Galloping Horse (detail)

FRONTISPIECE
139 Pottery figure of a squatting woman (detail)

PAGES x AND xi
218 - 234 Bronze chariots, horses, and warriors
unearthed at Wuwei (detail)

CONTENTS

THE EXHIBITS

Numerals refer to exhibit numbers

COMMITTEES

THE WORKING COMMITTEE FOR THE EXHIBITION
OF THE ARCHAEOLOGICAL FINDS OF THE
PEOPLE'S REPUBLIC OF CHINA OF THE
ASIAN ART MUSEUM OF SAN FRANCISCO, CALIFORNIA

The Honorable Joseph L. Alioto
Mayor of San Francisco
Honorary Chairman

Cyril Magnin
Chairman

William E. Goetze
Chairman
Asian Art Commission

Alexander D. Calhoun, Jr.
Vice-Chairman, Asian Art Foundation,
and Vice-Chairman, Asian Art Commission

George Hopper Fitch
Asian Art Commissioner

R. Gwin Follis
Asian Art Commissioner

James M. Gerstley
Vice-Chairman and Treasurer,
Asian Art Foundation, and
Vice-Chairman,
Asian Art Commission

William P. Scott, Jr.
Asian Art Commissioner

Mrs. Robert Seller
Asian Art Commissioner

Mrs. Walter Shorenstein
Asian Art Commissioner

René-Yvon Lefebvre d'Argencé
Director and Chief Curator
Asian Art Museum of San Francisco

Lorrie Bunker
Public Relations Director
Asian Art Museum of San Francisco

Anthony Garino
Administrative Assistant
Asian Art Museum of San Francisco

Clarence F. Shangraw
Senior Curator
Asian Art Museum of San Francisco

Diana Turner
Curator of Education
Asian Art Museum of San Francisco

Laurence Sickman
Director
The Nelson Gallery-Atkins Museum

Marc F. Wilson
Curator of Oriental Art
The Nelson Gallery-Atkins Museum

J. Carter Brown
Director
National Gallery of Art

John Barcroft
Program Director
Division of Public Programs
National Endowment for the Humanities

Alex B. Lacy
Deputy Director
Division of Public Programs
National Endowment for the Humanities

ASIAN ART COMMISSION
SAN FRANCISCO, CALIFORNIA

Commissioners

William E. Goetze
Chairman

Mrs. George T. Brady, Jr.

Alexander D. Calhoun, Jr.

Allen D. Christensen

Ransom M. Cook

Jack M. Dant

George Hopper Fitch

R. Gwin Follis

James M. Gerstley

Richard Gump

Mrs. Adrian Gruhn

R. V. Grady

Dr. S. I. Hayakawa

Jaquelin H. Hume

George F. Jewett, Jr.

Dr. J. Hardin Jones

Mrs. Albert E. Kern, Jr.

Dr. L. S. Kimbrough

Dr. T. Kong Lee

Cyril Magnin

Edward M. Nagel

Mrs. Richard R. Pettit

Mrs. Earl R. Rouda

William P. Scott, Jr.

Mrs. Robert Seller

Mrs. Walter Shorenstein

Dr. Haydn Williams

FOREWORD

A few years ago, word reached this country of the recent extraordinary archaeological discoveries that had been made throughout The People's Republic of China - finds that were not only of great archaeological interest but often of incomparable beauty. These exceptional objects, spanning some 600,000 years of China's past, have been shown in Washington and Kansas City and are now on display in the Asian Art Museum of San Francisco.

For this rare privilege, we wish to express our profound thanks and gratitude to the people and the Government of The People's Republic of China who, in their deep concern with the preservation and display of their country's cultural heritage, have so generously lent to the American public these newly excavated national treasures.

Many people were involved in the realization of this exhibition, and we owe each our deep appreciation for their generous expenditure of time and effort. The names of many of them are to be found on those committees listed elsewhere in this catalogue.

We are particularly grateful to the Committee for the Organization of Exhibitions of Archaeological Finds of The People's Republic of China. This committee selected the objects for the exhibition, and was of invaluable aid during its early planning stages. We should like to record our gratitude to the Chinese Exhibition Council of London for much assistance, and particularly to its chairman, Lord Trevelyan.

To all those countries which have played host to the exhibition - France, England, Austria, Sweden, and Canada - and to those who have worked with us to make the exhibition a reality, must go our sincere appreciation.

We are very grateful to the National Endowment for the Humanities and various local sponsors (listed on a separate page in this catalogue) for their generous support of our undertaking.

The National Gallery of Art, The Nelson Gallery-Atkins Museum and the Asian Art Museum of San Francisco are proud and honored to bring to you The Exhibition of Archaeological Finds of The People's Republic of China. We commend it to your interest and pleasure.

René-Yvon Lefebvre d'Argencé
Director and Chief Curator
Asian Art Museum of San Francisco

Laurence Sickman
Director
The Nelson Gallery-Atkins Museum

J. Carter Brown
Director
National Gallery of Art

COMPARATIVE CHRONOLOGY

CHINA	WESTERN AND OTHER
PRIMITIVE SOCIETY (c. 600,000-4,000 BC) Lantian Man (c. 600,000 BC)	Pebble-tool Culture } Heidelberg Man } (c. 600,000 BC) Neanderthal Man (c. 200,000 BC) Cro-Magnon Man (c. 35,000 BC)
SLAVE SOCIETY (c. 21st century-475 BC)	Great Pyramids in Egypt (c. 2500 BC)
HSIA DYNASTY (c. 21st-16th c. BC)	
SHANG DYNASTY (c. 16th-11th c. BC)	Stonehenge (c. 2000-1400 BC) Trojan War (c. 1200 BC)
WESTERN CHOU (c. 11th c.-770 BC)	Homer (8th c. BC)
SPRING AND AUTUMN PERIOD (c. 770-476 BC)	Rome founded (? 753 BC)
FEUDAL SOCIETY (475 BC-1840 AD)	
WARRING STATES PERIOD (475-221 BC)	Buddha (c. 560-c. 480 BC) Plato (c. 428-347 BC) Aristotle (c. 384-322 BC) Alexander the Great (336-323 BC)
CHIN DYNASTY (221-207 BC) Capital at Hsienyang (near Sian)	Hannibal crosses the Alps (218 BC)
WESTERN HAN DYNASTY (206 BC-24 AD) Capital at Changan (Sian)	Julius Caesar (? 104-44 BC)
EASTERN HAN DYNASTY (25-220 AD) Capital at Loyang	Jesus Christ (? 4 BC-30 AD)
THE THREE KINGDOMS (220-265 AD) *Wei* (220-265 AD) Capital at Loyang *Shu* (221-263 AD) Capital at Chengtu *Wu* (222-280 AD) Capital at Chienyeh (Nanking)	
WESTERN TSIN DYNASTY (265-316 AD) Capital at Loyang	Partition of Roman Empire (285 AD)
EASTERN TSIN DYNASTY (317-420 AD) Capital at Chienkang (Nanking)	Rome adopts Christianity (340 AD)
SOUTHERN DYNASTIES (420-589 AD) Capital at Chienkang (Nanking)	
NORTHERN DYNASTIES (386-581 AD) *Northern Wei Dynasty* (386-534 AD) Capital at Tatung, later at Loyang *Eastern Wei Dynasty* (534-549 AD) Capital at Yeh (Anyang)	Sack of Rome (410 AD)

CHINA	WESTERN AND OTHER
Western Wei Dynasty (535-556 AD) Capital at Changan (Sian)	
Northern Chi Dynasty (550-577 AD) Capital at Yeh (Anyang)	Silkworms introduced into Europe (552 AD)
Northern Chou Dynasty (557-581 AD) Capital at Changan (Sian)	Mohammed (570-632 AD)
SUI DYNASTY (581-618 AD) Capital at Tahsing (Sian)	
TANG DYNASTY (618-907 AD) Capital at Changan (Sian)	Charlemagne (768-814 AD)
FIVE DYNASTIES (907-960 AD)	
SUNG DYNASTY (960-1279 AD) *Northern Sung Dynasty* (960-1127 AD) Capital at Kaifeng *Southern Sung Dynasty* (1127-1279 AD) Capital at Linan (Hangchow)	Leif Ericsson (1000 AD) Norman Conquest of England (1066 AD) Paper first manufactured in Europe (1150 AD) Magna Carta (1215 AD)
LIAO DYNASTY (916-1125 AD) Capital at Linhuang (Barin Left Banner)	
KIN DYNASTY (1115-1234 AD) Capital at Huining (Acheng)	Genghis Khan (1206-1227 AD)
YUAN DYNASTY (1271-1368 AD) Capital at Tatu (Peking)	Gunpowder introduced in Europe (1313 AD)
MING DYNASTY (1368-1644 AD) Capital at Nanking, later at Peking	
CHING DYNASTY (1644-1840 AD, down to the 20th year of the reign of Taokuang) Capital at Peking	

CLASSIFICATION OF BRONZE VESSELS

Principal types of ceremonial vessels with their neolithic ceramic antecedent forms together with the appropriate old characters and their modern equivalents

Vessels for	Food					Water	
Type	li	ting	hsien	kuei	tou	p'an	chien
Primary form							
Old character and modern equivalent	鬲	鼎	甗	簋	豆	盤	監
Neolithic antecedent form							

Prepared for the exhibit in Vienna, based on the research of William Willets, Das Buch der Chinesischen Kunst, Dusseldorf-Wien, 1968, p. 96-f.

				Wine				
yu	hu	lei	fang-yi	chia	chüeh	ku	ho	kuang
卣	壺	罍	彝	斚	爵		盉	

COLOR PLATES

29

36

70

80

89

87

95

102

145

168

265 — 272

274

277

337

369

370

EXHIBITS

I / Excavations of the Sites of Lantian Man and Peking Man

(about 600,000—400,000 years ago)

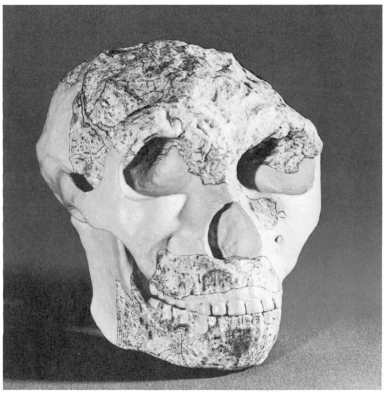

1

1. Skull and lower jaw of
   Lantian Man (model)
   Cranium: Unearthed in 1964 at
                Kungwangling village,
                Lantian, Shensi
   Lower jaw: Unearthed in 1963 at
                Chenchiawo village,
                Lantian, Shensi

2. Bust of Lantian Man
   (restoration)
   Made in 1972 by the Institute of
   Vertebrate Palentology and
   Paleoanthropology of the
   Chinese Academy of Sciences

2

3

4

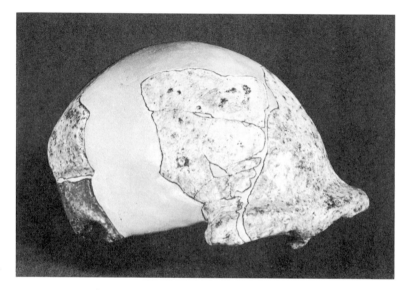

5

3. Pointed tool of quartzite
   (used by Lantian man)
   (reproduction)
   Length 17.5 cm.
   Unearthed in 1965 at Kungwangling village,
   Lantian, Shensi

4. Scraper of vein quartz
   (used by Lantian man)
   (reproduction)
   Length 2.8 cm.
   Unearthed in 1965 at Kungwangling village,
   Lantian Shensi

5. Skull of Peking Man (model)
   Unearthed in 1966 at Locality I of
   Choukoutien, Peking

6. Lower jaw of Peking Man (model)
   Unearthed in 1959 at Locality I
   of Choukoutien, Peking

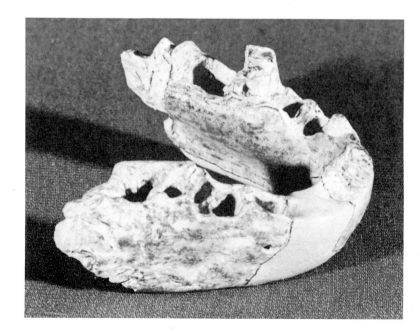

6

Tools used by Peking Man and evidence of use of fire by Peking Man, unearthed in 1966 at Locality I of Choukoutien, Peking

7

12

8

13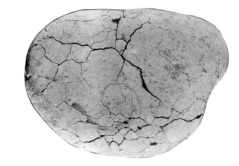

9

10

7. Stone hammer
   Length 8.2 cm.

8. Flint scraper
   Length 13.2 cm.

9. Flint scraper
   Length 8.6 cm.

10. Scraper of vein quartz
    Length 4.5 cm.

11. Burnt earth
    Length 24 cm.

12. Burnt bone
    Length 11 cm.

13. Burnt stone
    Length 8.5 cm.

11

II / Yangshao Culture Site at Panpo Village,
Sian, Shensi Province, Unearthed between 1954 and 1957
(about 6,000 years ago)

Panpo Village during excavation

14

15

14. Stone axe
Length 12 cm.

15. Stone chisel
Length 8 cm.

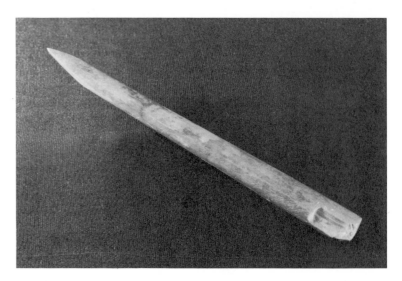

17

16

16. Stone adze
    Length 6 cm.

17. Bone spade
    Length 11 cm.

18. Bone chisel .
    Length 14 cm.

19. Bone harpoon head
    Length 14.8 cm.

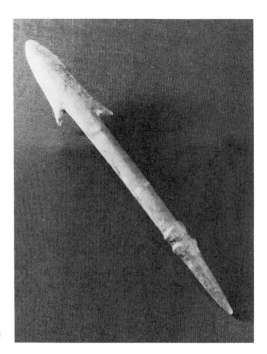

18

19

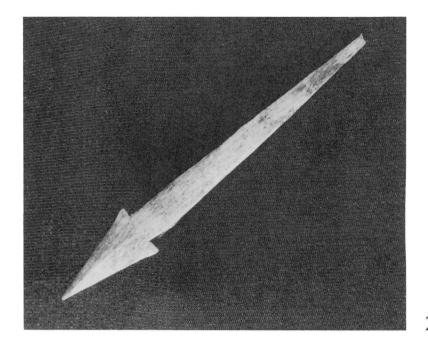

20. Bone arrow head
    Length 6.1 cm.

21. Bone hairpin
    Length 16 cm.

22. Bone needle
    Length 16.5 cm.

20

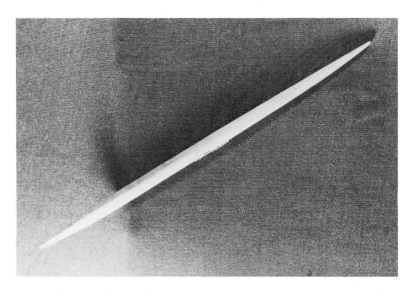

21

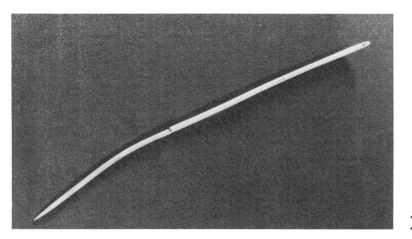

22

23

24

23. Stone whorl
    Diameter 3.8 cm.

24. Pottery bowl (with textile impressions
    on bottom)
    Height 4 cm., dia. of mouth 13 cm.

25. Pottery bowl (with matting impressions
    on bottom)
    Height 10.5 cm., dia. of mouth 24 cm.

25

26

27

26. Pottery jar with stippling
    Height 11 cm.

27. Pottery jar with finger-nail
    impressions
    Height 15 cm.

28

30

29

28. Pottery amphora with pointed bottom
Height 43 cm.

29. Pottery basin painted with human-mask design
Height 17 cm., dia. of mouth 44.5 cm.

30. Pottery basin painted with deer design
Height 17 cm., dia. of mouth 42.8 cm.

31. Pottery bowl painted with triangle design
    Height 9 cm., dia. of mouth 14.5 cm.

32. Pottery jar painted with triangle design
    Height 12.7 cm.

33

33. Painted pottery waisted jar
    Height 18.3 cm.
    Unearthed in 1958 at Lanchow, Kansu

34. Painted pottery *tou* (stemmed bowl) with wave design
Height 16.4 cm.
Unearthed in 1958 at Lanchow, Kansu

35. Pottery basin painted with curved lines
Height 9.5 cm., dia. of mouth 23 cm.
Unearthed in 1966 at Lanchow, Kansu

34

35

36. Painted pottery amphora with
flat bottom
Height 38 cm.
Unearthed in 1958 at
Kanku, Kansu

37. Painted pottery vase with four circles filled
in with geometric pattern
Height 49 cm.
Unearthed in 1956 at Yungching, Kansu

37

38

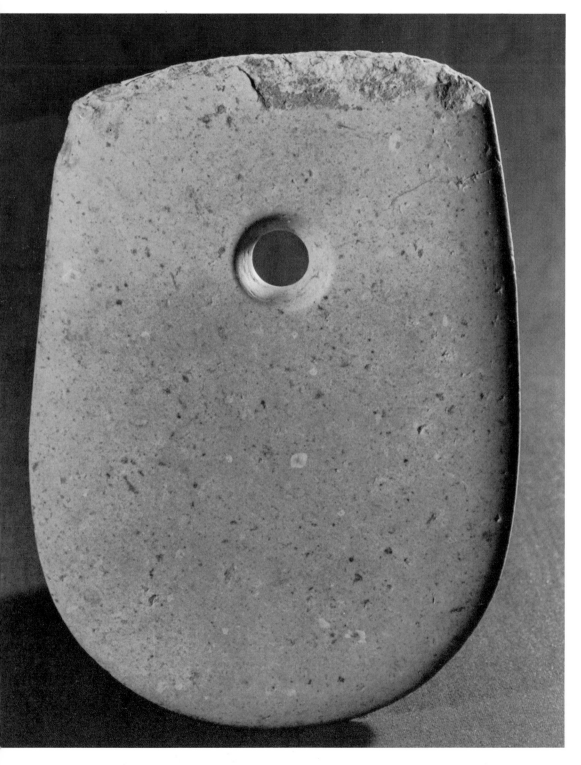

38. Perforated stone axe
Length 15 cm.
Unearthed in 1956 at
Nanking, Kiangsu

39

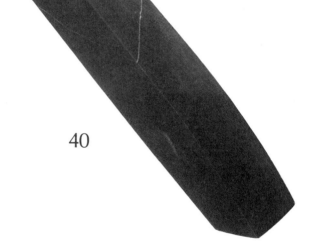

40

41. Stone knife with seven holes
    Length 22.6 cm.
    Unearthed in 1956 at Nanking, Kiangsu

40. Stone stepped adze
    Length 17.3 cm.
    Unearthed in 1953 at Wuhsien, Kiangsu

41. Stone hoe
    Length 13.5 cm.
    Unearthed in 1955 at Nanking, Kiangsu

41

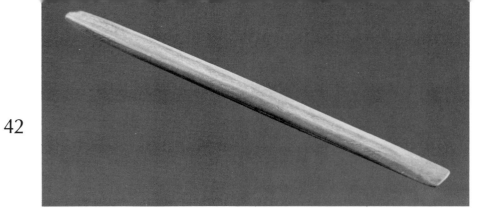

42

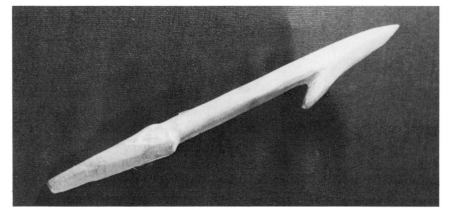

43

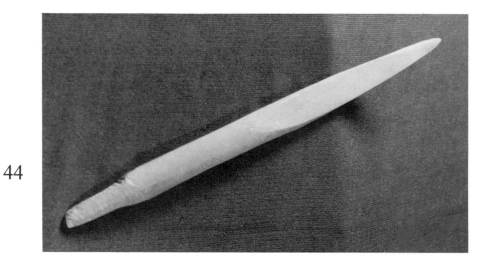

44

42. Bone chisel
    Length 16.3 cm.
    Unearthed in 1960 at Wukiang, Kiangsu

43. Bone harpoon
    Length 16.5 cm.
    Unearthed in 1960 at Wukiang, Kiangsu

44. Bone arrow head
    Length 16 cm.
    Unearthed in 1960 at Wukiang, Kiangsu

45. Bone needle
    Length 18.1 cm.
    Unearthed in 1960 at Wukiang, Kiangsu

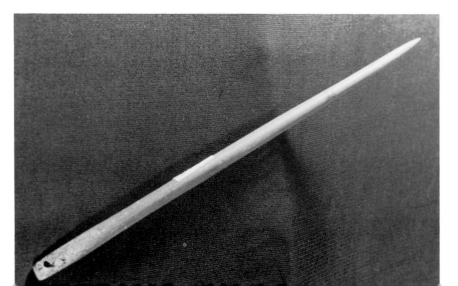

45

46. *Chueh* ring (penannular) of white jade
Diameter 6.2 cm.
Unearthed in 1956 at Nanking, Kiangsu

47. *Huang* (half-ring) of green nephrite
Length 12.6 cm.
Unearthed in 1955 at Nanking, Kiangsu

48. Painted pottery bowl
Height 10 cm., dia. of mouth 18 cm.
Unearthed in 1966 at Peihsien, Kiangsu

46

47

48

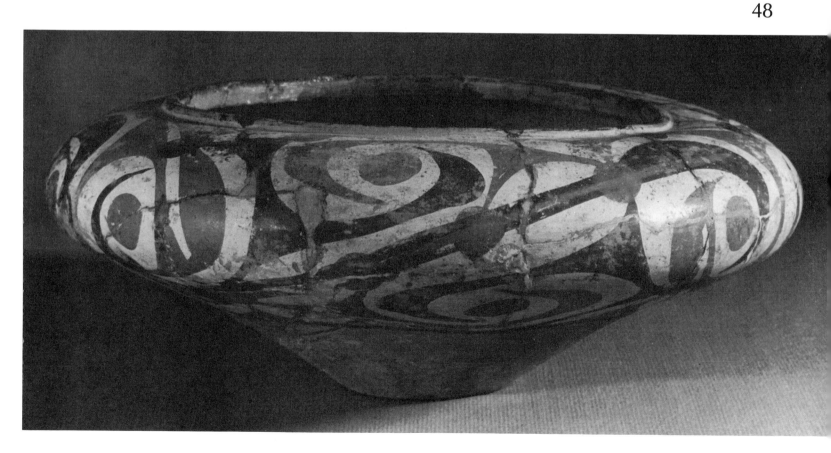

49. Painted pottery vase with flower-petal design
Height 19.5 cm.
Unearthed in 1966 at Peihsien, Kiangsu

50. Pottery basin painted with flower-petal design
Height 16.5 cm., dia. of mouth 30.2 cm.
Unearthed in 1966 at Peihsien, Kiangsu

49

50

51. Pottery basin painted with eight-point
    star design
    Height 18.5 cm., dia. of mouth 33.8 cm.
    Unearthed in 1963 at Peihsien, Kiangsu

51

52. Red pottery tripod *kuei* (pitcher)
    Height 31.8 cm.
    Unearthed in 1960

53. White pottery tripod *kuei* (pitcher)
    Height 29.7 cm.
    Unearthed in 1960

52

53

54. White pottery *ho* (kettle)
Height 31 cm.
Unearthed in 1964

55

56

55. Black pottery cup with two ears
   Height 12.5 cm.
   Unearthed in 1960

56. Black pottery *tou* (stemmed cup) with thin body
   Height 16.3 cm.
   Unearthed in 1960

58

57. Black pottery tripod *ting*
    Height 15 cm.
    Unearthed in 1960

58. Black pottery stemmed plate
    Height 18.7 cm., dia. 43.8 cm.
    Unearthed in 1960

57

SHANG DYNASTY
(16th - 11th century B.C.)

VI / Shang Dynasty Site at Chengchow, Honan Province
(16th - 11th century B.C.)

59. Bronze *ko* with whorl design
    Length 20.3 cm.
    Unearthed in 1954

60. Bronze spear head
    Length 18.5 cm.
    Unearthed in 1954

60

59

61

62

64

63

61. Bronze arrow head
    Length 6.7 cm.
    Unearthed in 1953

62. Bronze arrow head
    Length 6.5 cm.
    Unearthed in 1954

63. Bronze knife
    Length 25.6 cm.
    Unearthed in 1954

64. Dark green nephrite *ko* (halberd)
    Length 38 cm.
    Unearthed in 1955

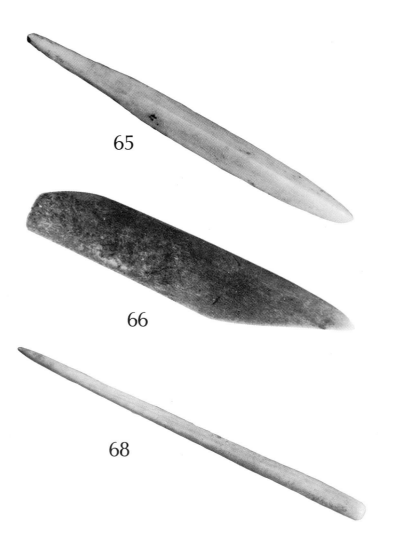

69

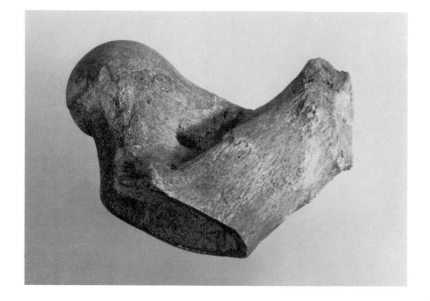

65. Bone arrow head
    Length 9.5 cm.
    Unearthed in 1955

66. Bone *pi* (spatula)
    Length 11 cm.
    Unearthed in 1954

67. Bone comb
    Length 10.1 cm.
    Unearthed in 1954

68. Bone hairpin
    Length 15.3 cm.
    Unearthed in 1955

69. Thigh bone of an ox
    sawed for making artifacts
    Length 14 cm.
    Unearthed in 1955

70. Bronze *lei* with animal-mask
    design
    Height 25 cm.
    Unearthed in 1955

71. Bronze tripod *chia* with animal-mask design
    Height 22 cm.
    Unearthed in 1955

72. Bronze tripod *ting* with animal-mask design
    Height 19 cm.
    Unearthed in 1955

71

72

73. Bronze *pan* with *kuei* dragon design
    Height 10.5 cm., dia. of mouth 30 cm.
    Unearthed in 1955

73

74

74. Bronze *tsun* with animal-mask design
    Height 24.9 cm.
    Unearthed in 1954

75. Bronze tripod *li* with *kuei* dragon design
    Height 16.5 cm.
    Unearthed in 1955

75

76

76. Bronze *ku* with animal-mask design
    Height 18 cm.
    Unearthed in 1965

77. Bronze *chueh* with animal-mask design
    Height 17.2 cm.
    Unearthed in 1965

77

78. Large mouthed *tsun*
    (wine container) of proto-porcelain
    Height 28.2 cm.
    Unearthed in 1965

79. Pottery *yen*
Height 40 cm.
Unearthed in 1953

80. Pottery *tsun*
Height 34.5 cm.
Unearthed in 1954

79

80

82

81. Bronze *yu,* inscribed "Pei Kan (?)"
    12th century B.C.
    Height including handle 29 cm.
    Unearthed in 1950 from the large tomb at Wukuan
    village, Anyang, Honan

82. Bronze *kuei,* inscribed "Pei Kan (?) Ko"
    12th century B.C.
    Height 14.3 cm., dia. of mouth 20.7 cm.
    Unearthed in 1950 from the large tomb at Wukuan
    village, Anyang, Honan

83

83. Bronze tripod *ting*, inscribed "Fu Chi"
    11th century B.C.
    Height 21.7 cm.
    Unearthed in 1950 at Anyang, Honan

84. Bronze tripod *chia*, inscribed
"Mu Ya"
12th century B.C.
Height 30.8 cm.
Unearthed in 1959 at Anyang,
Honan

84

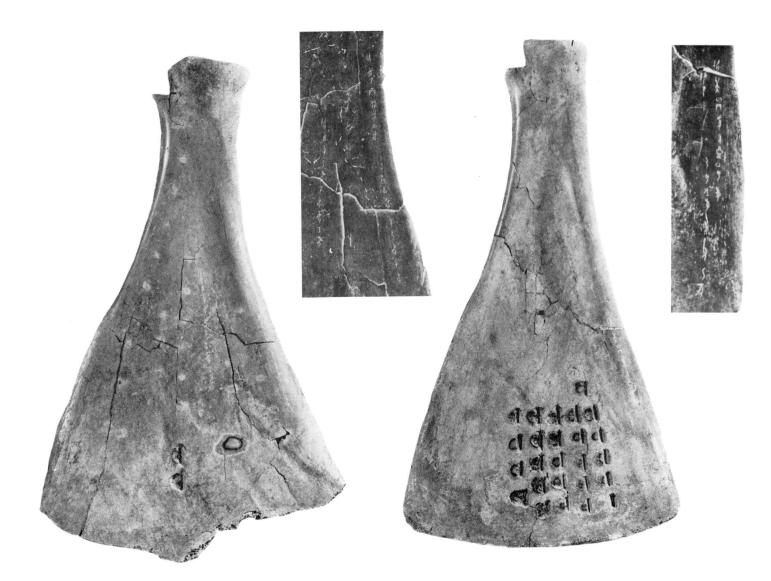

85

86

85. Inscription on ox shoulder blade
14th century B.C.
Length 40.5 cm.
Unearthed in 1971 at Anyang, Honan

86. Inscription on ox shoulder blade
14th century B.C.
Length 37 cm.
Unearthed in 1971 at Anyang, Honan

FRONT VIEW

87. Owl-shaped bronze *yu*
11th century B.C.
Height 19.7 cm.
Unearthed in 1957 at Shihlou, Shansi

87

SIDE VIEW

88

88. Bronze *kuang* with dragon design
11th century B.C.
Length 41.5 cm.
Unearthed in 1959 at Shihlou, Shansi

88 B

88. Bronze *kuang* with dragon design
11th century B.C.
Length 41.5 cm.
Unearthed in 1959 at Shihlou, Shansi

88 C

89. Bronze *tsun* with animal-mask design
    12th — 11th century B.C.
    Height 47 cm.
    Unearthed in 1957 at Funan, Anhwei

90. Bronze tripod *chia* with animal-mask
    design
    12th century B.C.
    Height 55.3 cm.
    Unearthed in 1965 at Feihsi, Anhwei

91. Bronze *ting* with human-mask design, inscribed "Ta Ho"
11th century B.C.
Height 38.7 cm.
Unearthed in 1959 at Ninghsiang, Hunan

92. Bronze square *tsun* with animal-mask decoration
11th century B.C.
Height 53.8 cm.
Unearthed in 1963 at Changning, Hunan

91

IX / Western Chou Bronzes from Chichia Village,
Fufeng, Shensi Province
(10th — 9th century B.C.)

93

93. Bronze *kuang* marked "Jih Chi"
    10th century B.C.
    Height 31.6 cm.
    Unearthed in 1963

94. Bronze square *tsun* marked "Jih Chi"
    10th century B.C.
    Height 29.5 cm.
    Unearthed in 1963

94

作文考日己寶
尊宗彝其子孫
萬年永寶用大

95. Bronze square *yi* marked "Jih
10th century B.C.
Height 38.5 cm.
Unearthed in 1963

96. Bronze *ho* with bird-shaped lid
     10th century B.C.
     Height 38 cm.
     Unearthed in 1963

97. Bronze *hu* marked "Chi Fu"
10th — 9th century B.C.
Height 59.4 cm.
Unearthed in 1960

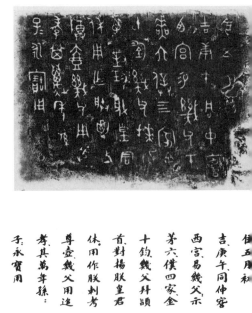

隹五月初
吉庚午同仲客
西宮易幾父示
茅六樸易四家金
十鈞幾父升頡
首對揚朕皇君
休用作朕刺考
尊壺幾用逆
羞其萬年孫：
子永寶用

98. Bronze *lei* with *kuei* dragon design
    10th — 9th century B.C.
    Height 46.1 cm.
    Unearthed in 1960

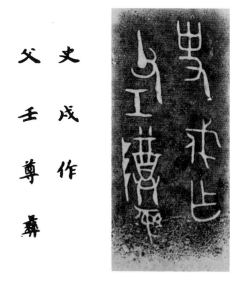

父　史
壬　戊
尊　作
彝

99. Bronze *kuei* marked "Yu Fu Kuei"
    Height 16.7 cm., dia. of mouth 25 cm.

100. Bronze *yu* marked "Shih Hsu"
     Height including handle 28.5 cm.

100

99

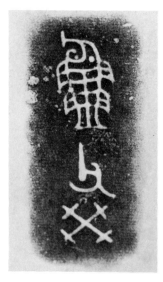

101. Bronze *yu* marked "Kung"
Height including handle 23.5 cm.
Unearthed in 1965

101

公作寶尊彝
其孫子永用

102. Bronze *kuei* decorated with
     stylized animal-mask design
     Height 19.7 cm., dia. of mouth 27.2 cm.
     Unearthed in 1965

103

103. Bronze *pan* with *kuei* dragon design
Height 9.4 cm., dia. of mouth 31.6 cm.
Unearthed in 1959

104

105

104. Proto-porcelain vase with three ears
     Height 11 cm.
     Unearthed in 1965

105. Proto-porcelain *tsun* (wine vessel) with two ears
     Height 11.9 cm.
     Unearthed in 1965

106. Proto-porcelain vase with two ears
     Height 15 cm.
     Unearthed in 1965

106

春
秋

THE SPRING AND AUTUMN PERIOD
(770 — 475 B.C.)

XII / Bronzes of the Spring and Autumn Period from Anhwei and Shansi Provinces
(5th century B.C.)

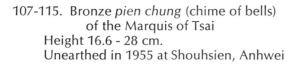

107-115. Bronze *pien chung* (chime of bells)
of the Marquis of Tsai
Height 16.6 - 28 cm.
Unearthed in 1955 at Shouhsien, Anhwei

116. Bronze tripod *ting* in the shape of a sacrificial animal
Height 27.5 cm.
Unearthed in 1959 at Shucheng, Anhwei

117

117. Bronze rectangular *hu* with interlaced dragon design
Height 86.6 cm.
Unearthed in 1961 at Houma, Shansi

118. Bronze *chien* with interlaced hydras design
Height 36.8 cm., dia. of mouth 76 cm.
Unearthed in 1961 at Houma, Shansi

118

XIII / Surverys and Excavations of City Sites of the Warring States Period
(4th century B.C.)

119

119. Bronze knocker ornamented
     with interlaced hydras and
     phoenix design
     Length of animal mask 45.5 cm.,
     dia. of ring 29 cm.
     Unearthed in 1966 at Yihsien,
     Hopei

121

120. Semi-cylindrical tile with cicada pattern
Length 54.5 cm.
Unearthed in 1966 at Yihsien, Hopei

121. Semi-circular tile-end with animal-mask design
Length 33.5 cm., dia. 23 cm.
Unearthed in 1964 at Yihsien, Hopei

122. Semi-circular tile-end with animal-mask design
Length 14 cm., dia. 28 cm.
Unearthed in 1964 at Yihsien, Hopei

120

122

XIV / Iron-Casting Moulds, Unearthed in 1953 at Hsinglung, Hopei Province
(4th century B.C.)

123

124

123. Iron mould and core for casting an axe, inscribed "Right Granary"
Length of mould 28.6 cm., length of core 21.9 cm.

124. Iron mould for casting a pair of sickles, inscribed "Right Granary"
Length 32.5 cm.

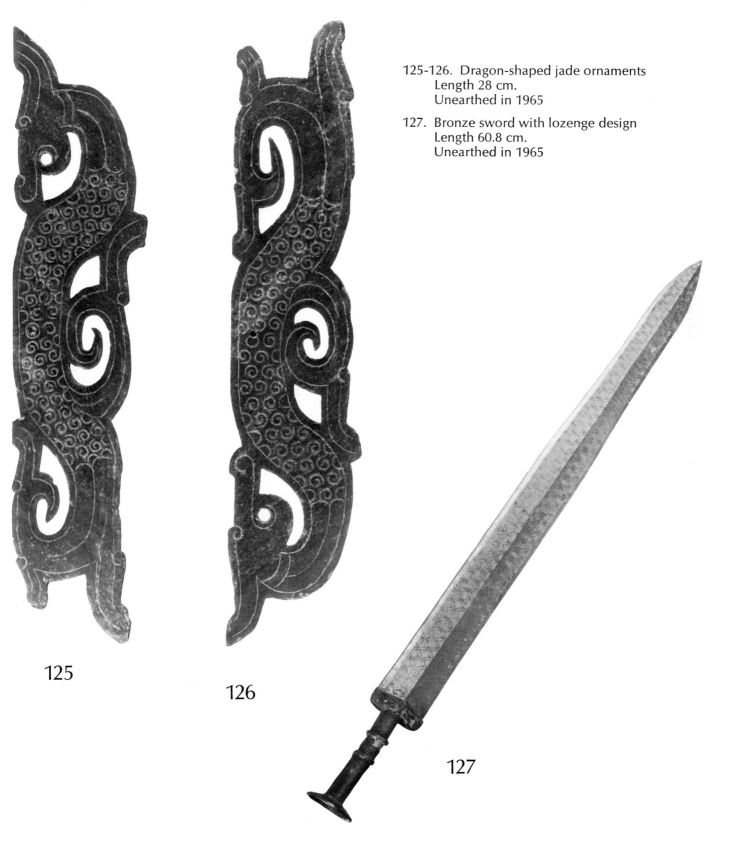

125-126. Dragon-shaped jade ornaments
   Length 28 cm.
   Unearthed in 1965

127. Bronze sword with lozenge design
   Length 60.8 cm.
   Unearthed in 1965

125

126

127

128. Bronze *tsun* (wine vessel)
with stylized dragon design
Height 17.1 cm.
Unearthed in 1965

129. Iron belt-hook with gold inlay
Length 46.3 cm.
Unearthed in 1965

128

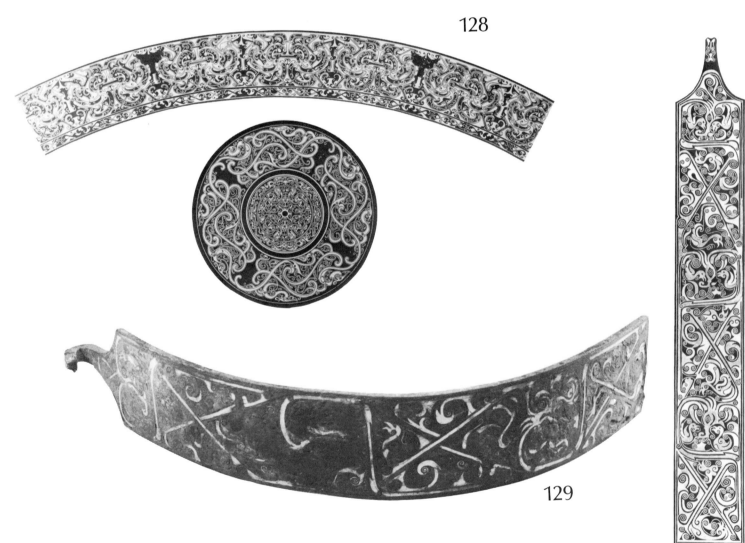

129

131

130. Pottery mould for casting a figure of a tiger
Length 18.5 cm.
Unearthed in 1959 at Houma, Shansi

131. Pottery model for making mould of animal-head
Height 10.9 cm.
Unearthed in 1960 at Houma, Shansi

130

132. Pottery relief model for making a mould of an
     animal-mask design
     Length 32.8 cm.
     Unearthed in 1960 at Houma, Shansi

133. Bronze *tou* inlaid with gold in *kuei* dragon design
     Height 19.2 cm.
     Unearthed in 1965 at Changchih, Shansi

134

134. Bronze rim of a vessel inlaid with gold and silver
Diameter 12 cm.
Unearthed in 1954 at Hochin, Shansi

135. Bronze ornament with silver inlay
Length 21.3 cm.
Unearthed in 1954 at Yungchi, Shansi

136. Bronze ewer with eagle's head
Height 47.5 cm.
Unearthed in 1970 at Chucheng, Shant

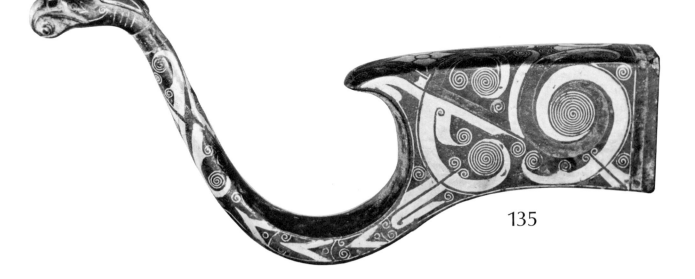

135

CHIN DYNASTY
(221 — 207 B.C.)

XVII / Cultural Relics of the Chin Dynasty from Shensi and Shantung Provinces
(3rd century B.C.)

137

138

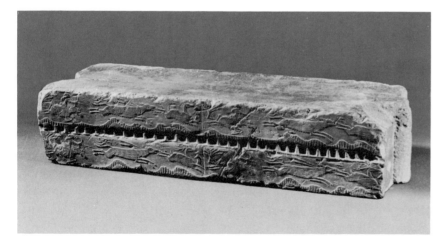

137. Pottery measure, inscribed
Height 9.4 cm., dia. of mouth 20.4 cm.
Unearthed in 1963 at Tsouhsien, Shantung

138. Brick stamped with a hunting scene
Length 47.5 cm.
Unearthed in 1957 at Lintung, Shensi

139. Pottery figure of a squatting woman
Height 64.5 cm.
Unearthed in 1964 at Lintung, Shensi

139

XVIII / The Tombs of Liu Sheng, Prince Ching of Chungshan, of the Western Han Dynasty and of His Wife, Tou Wan, unearthed in 1968 at Mancheng, Hopei Province

Central chamber of Liu Sheng's tomb

140. Bronze *chuan* (water container) inscribed "Household of the Prince of Chungshan" Height 13 cm., dia. of mouth 28.1 cm. Unearthed from the tomb of Tou Wan

141

Section of bird script inlay redrawn

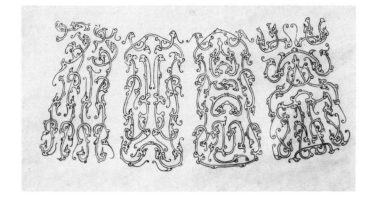

141. Bronze *hu* (wine vessel) with gold and silver inlay of
bird script
Height 40 cm.
Unearthed from the tomb of Tou Wan

142

142. Bronze *hu* (wine vessel) inlaid with gold and silver
Height 59 cm.
Unearthed from the tomb of Liu Sheng

143. Bronze lamp in the form of a ram
Height of ram 18.6 cm., length 23 cm.
Unearthed from the tomb of Liu Sheng

143

145

144. Bronze lamp with stand inscribed "Household of Prince of Chungshan" Height of lamp 5.2 cm., dia. of stand 22.1 cm. Unearthed from the tomb of Tou Wan

145. Bronze lamp with shade Height 32.8 cm. Unearthed from the tomb of Liu Sheng

144

146. Bronze *poshan* censer
supported by a human
figure mounted on a
beast
Height 32.4 cm.
Unearthed from the
tomb of Tou Wan

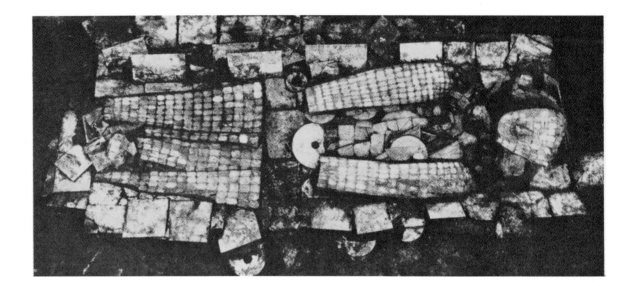

147

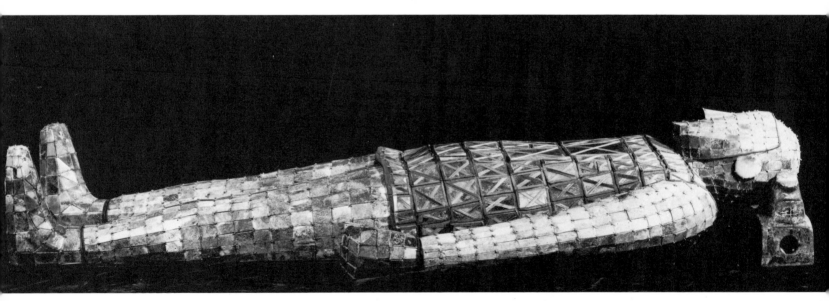

147. Jade suit, sewn with gold thread; shroud
for Tou Wan, wife of Prince Ching of
Chungshan
Length 172 cm.
Unearthed from the tomb of Tou Wan

Detail, 147

148. Gilt bronze headrest inlaid
     with jade
     Length 41.3 cm.
     Unearthed from the tomb of
     Tou Wan

148

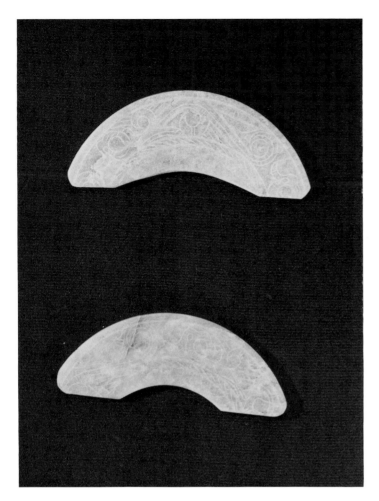

151

149, 150

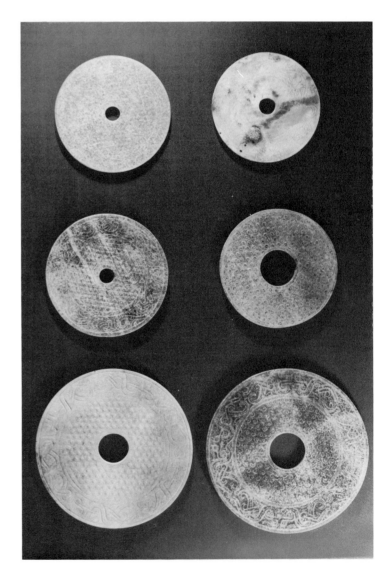

149, 150. Jade *huang* (crescent-shaped ritual object)
(2 pieces)
Length of smaller 13 cm., length of
larger 13.7 cm.
Unearthed from the tomb of Tou Wan

151. Tou Wan's bronze seal (reproduction)
2 cm. square, 0.7 cm. thick
Unearthed from the tomb of Tou Wan

152-157. Jade *pi* discs
Diameter 14.1 cm. — 21.2 cm.
Unearthed from the tomb of Tou Wan

152—157

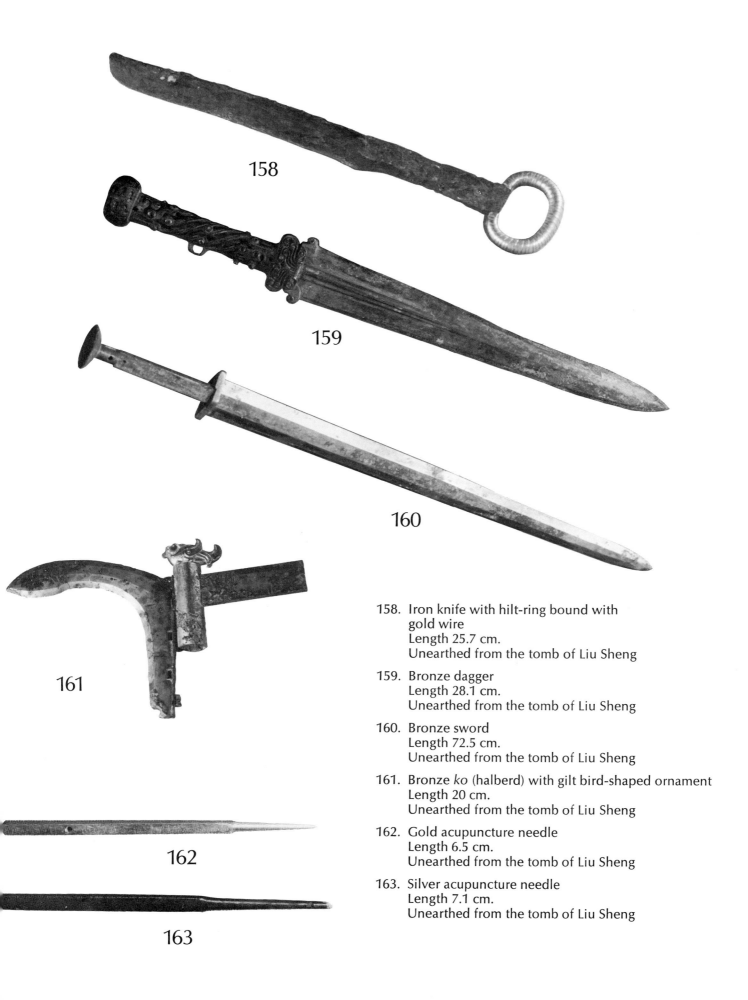

158. Iron knife with hilt-ring bound with
     gold wire
     Length 25.7 cm.
     Unearthed from the tomb of Liu Sheng

159. Bronze dagger
     Length 28.1 cm.
     Unearthed from the tomb of Liu Sheng

160. Bronze sword
     Length 72.5 cm.
     Unearthed from the tomb of Liu Sheng

161. Bronze *ko* (halberd) with gilt bird-shaped ornament
     Length 20 cm.
     Unearthed from the tomb of Liu Sheng

162. Gold acupuncture needle
     Length 6.5 cm.
     Unearthed from the tomb of Liu Sheng

163. Silver acupuncture needle
     Length 7.1 cm.
     Unearthed from the tomb of Liu Sheng

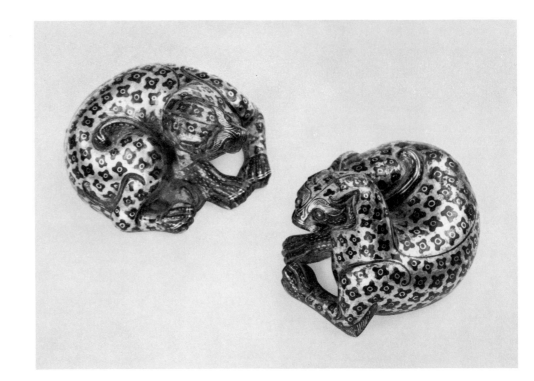

164

165

164, 165. Bronze leopards inlaid with gold
Height 3.5 cm.
Unearthed from the tomb of Liu Sheng

166, 167. Bronze feet of vessel in shape of bears
          and birds
          Height 11.4 cm. and 11.7 cm.
          Unearthed from the tomb of Liu Sheng

168. Pottery basin painted with fish design
     Height 14.7 cm., dia. of mouth 55.5 cm.
     Unearthed from the tomb of Liu Sheng

168

169. Bronze ploughshare
Length 30 cm.
Unearthed in 1956

169

170. Bronze axe ornamented
with two birds
Height 24 cm.
Unearthed in 1956

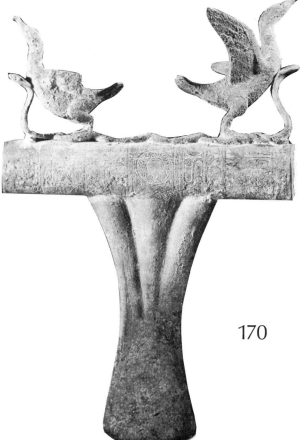

170

171. Bronze mandarin duck
Height 11.2 cm.
Unearthed in 1956

Detail, 172

171

172. Bronze cowrie-container decorated with
weaving scene on lid
Height 27.5 cm., dia. of bottom 30.9 cm.
Unearthed in 1955

173. Bronze ornament in form of
    buffalo heads and bulls
    Width 11.2 cm.
    Unearthed in 1956

174. Bronze ornament in form of
    boar struggling with two tigers
    Length 17.1 cm.
    Unearthed in 1956

173

174

175. Bronze deer
    Height 15.6 cm.
    Unearthed in 1956

176. Bronze peacock
    Height 14.4 cm.
    Unearthed in 1956

177—192

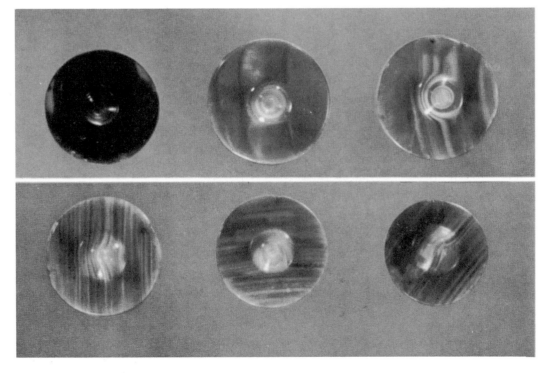

177-192. Agate and carnelian be[
Length 1.1 cm. - 7.3 cm.
Unearthed in 1956

193-198. Agate and carnelian
button-shaped
ornaments
Diameter 4.4 cm. - 5.8 cm.
Unearthed in 1956

193—198

199

199, 200. Two painted pottery horsemen
2nd century B.C.
Height 65 cm. and 68.5 cm.
Unearthed in 1965 at Hsienyang, Shensi

200

201. Bronze *fang hu* (square wine vessel) inlaid
     with gold in hydras design
     Height 61 cm.
     Unearthed in 1964 at Sian, Shensi

202. Silver-inlaid bronze *tsun* (wine vessel)
  in the form of a sacrificial animal
  2nd century B.C.
  Height 27.4 cm., length 41.8 cm.
  Unearthed in 1965 at Lienshui, Kiangsu

203

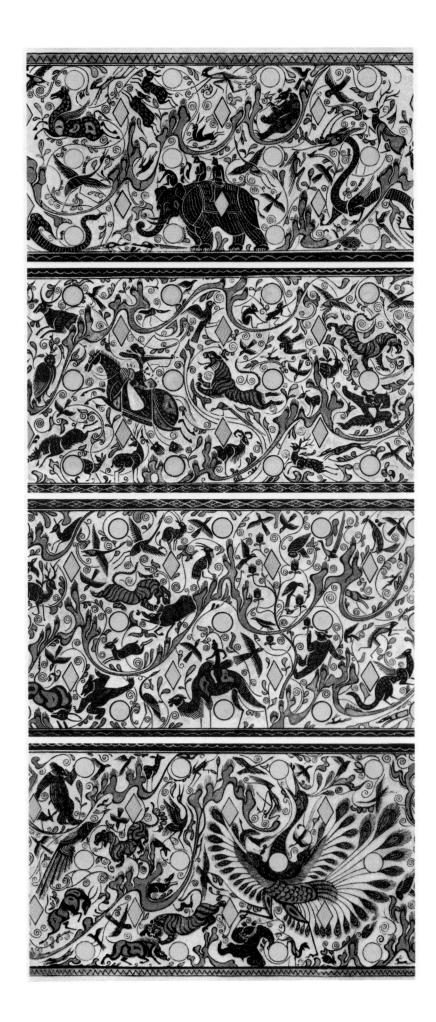

203. Bronze chariot ornament inlaid with
gold and silver
1st century B.C.
Length 26.5 cm.
Unearthed in 1965 at Tinghsien, Hopei

204. Bronze *tsun* (wine vessel) gilded and
with silver decoration, inscribed
26 B.C.
Height 34.7 cm., dia. of mouth 65.5 cm.
Unearthed in 1962 at Yuyu, Shansi

204

205

206

205. Gilded bronze *tsun* for warming wine
26 B.C.
Height 24.5 cm., dia. of mouth 23.4 cm.
Unearthed in 1962 at Yuyu, Shansi

206. Painted pottery vase
1st century B.C.
Height 49.5 cm.
Unearthed in 1957 at Loyang, Honan

207. Pottery model of a courtyard
1st century A.D.
Height 76 cm., width 93 cm.
Unearthed in 1959 at Chengchow, Honan

207

208. Painted wooden unicorn
    2nd century A.D.
    Height 38.5 cm., length 59 cm.
    Unearthed in 1959 at Wuwei, Kansu

209. Wooden monkey
    2nd century A.D.
    Height 32.5 cm.
    Unearthed in 1957 at Wuwei, Kansu

209

208

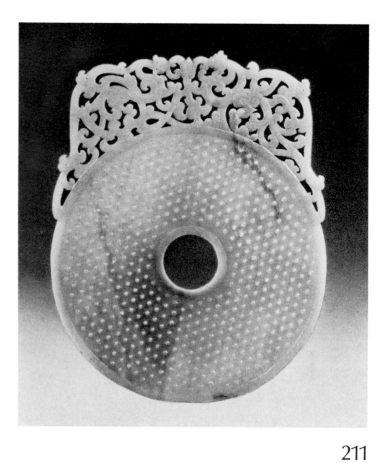

211

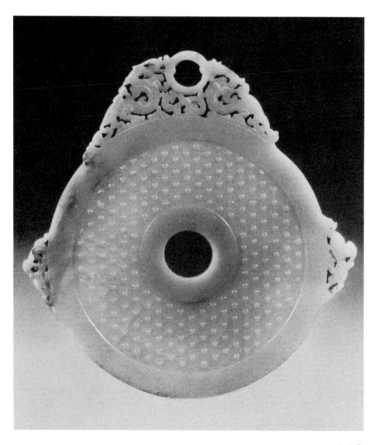

210

210. *Pi* disc of green nephrite decorated with animal design and ring
1st century A.D.
Height 30 cm.
Unearthed in 1969 at Tinghsien, Hopei

211. *Pi* disc of green nephrite decorated with hydras design
1st century A.D.
Height 25.5 cm.
Unearthed in 1959 at Tinghsien, Hopei

212 - 217. Six pottery figures of musicians and
            dancers
            1st century A.D.
            Height 15 cm. — 15.5 cm.
            Unearthed in 1965 at Loyang, Honan

218. Bronze galloping horse
Height 34.5 cm., length 45 cm.

218

219, 220. Two bronze horses
Height 36.5 cm. and 38 cm.

219, 220

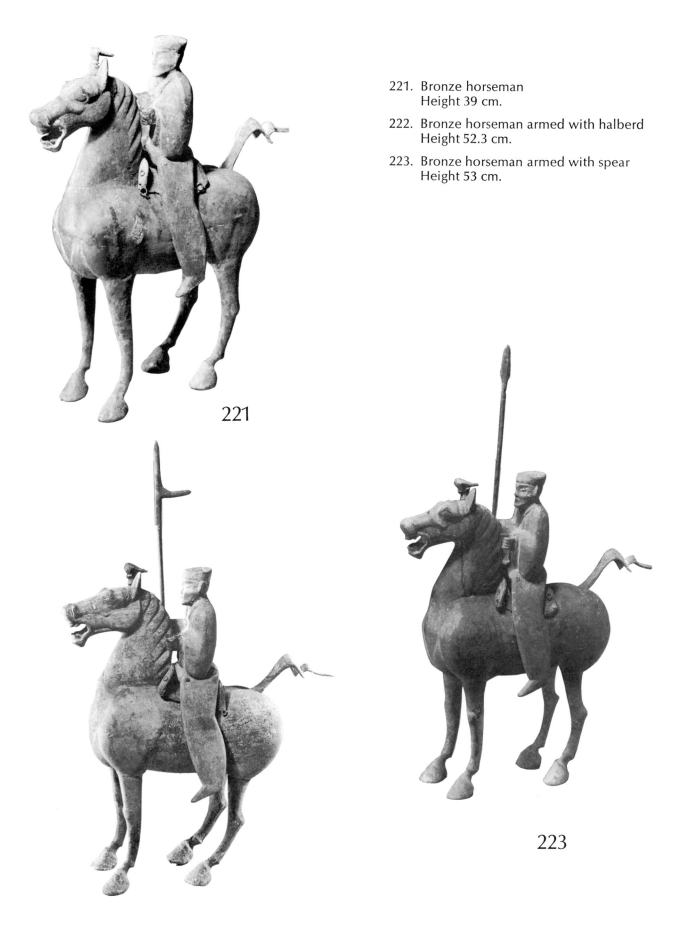

221. Bronze horseman
     Height 39 cm.

222. Bronze horseman armed with halberd
     Height 52.3 cm.

223. Bronze horseman armed with spear
     Height 53 cm.

221

222

223

228 — 231

224 - 227. Bronze chariot mounted
with ax (a chariot, a horse, and
two figurines)
Height of horse 40 cm., length
of chariot 33 cm.

228 - 231. Bronze yao chariot (a
chariot, a horse, and two
figurines)
Height of horse 40 cm., height
of chariot 43.5 cm.

224 — 227

232 - 234. Bronze *chu* cart (a cart, a horse, and a figurine)
Height of horse 38 cm., length of
cart 63 cm.

235. Procession scene, part of the wall-painting
of an Eastern Han tomb (copy)
170 x 327 cm.
Discovered in 1971 at Anping, Hopei

232 — 234

235

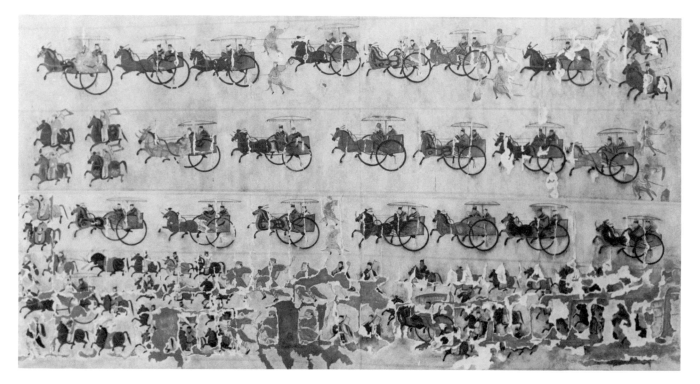

両晋南北朝

THE THREE KINGDOMS, THE WESTERN AND EASTERN TSIN, AND THE SOUTHERN AND NORTHERN DYNASTIES
(220 — 589 A.D.)

XXII / Ceramics of the Tsin and Southern and Northern Dynasties from Chekiang, Kiangsu, and Honan Provinces
(265 — 589 A.D.)

236

236. Celadon jar crowned with miniature buildings and human figures
Latter half of 3rd century A.D. (Western Tsin)
Height 46.6 cm.
Unearthed in 1965 at Shaohsing, Chekiang

237. Celadon vase in shape of an eagle
First half of 4th century A.D. (Western Tsin)
Height 17 cm.
Unearthed in 1964 at Nanking, Kiangsu

238

238. Celadon lion-shaped vessel
Latter half of 3rd century A.D. (Western Tsin)
Length 17.5 cm.
Unearthed in 1966 at Tanyang, Kiangsu

239. Celadon pot ornamented with the head of a cock
4th century A.D. (Eastern Tsin)
Height 23.5 cm.
Unearthed in 1967 at Yuyao, Chekiang

240. Celadon vase with dish mouth and eight rings
First half of 6th century A.D. (Southern Dynasties)
Height 26 cm.
Unearthed in 1964 at Juian, Chekiang

241

241. Celadon jar with incised design
Latter half of 6th century A.D. (Northern Chi)
Height 29 cm.
Unearthed in 1958 at Puyang, Honan

242. Yellowish green-glazed jar with dark green splashes
and four rings
Latter half of 6th century A.D. (Northern Chi)
Height 23.5 cm.
Unearthed in 1958 at Puyang, Honan.

243. Yellow-glazed flat flask decorated with musicians and dancers
Latter half of 6th century A.D. (Northern Chi)
Height 20.5 cm.
Unearthed in 1971 at Anyang, Honan

243

244. Stone carved with dragons and tigers
5th century A. D. (Northern Wei)
Height 16.5 cm., width 32 cm.
Unearthed in 1966 at Tatung, Shansi

245. Stone carved with figures of musicians,
dancers, dragons, and tigers
5th century A.D. (Northern Wei)
Height 16.5 cm., width 32.6 cm.
Unearthed in 1966 at Tatung, Shansi

244

245

246. Stone image of Sakyamuni in the act of preaching
     Latter half of 6th century A.D. (Northern Chi)
     Height 72.6 cm.
     Unearthed in 1958 at Linchang, Hopei

XXIV

Han to Tang Dynasty Cultural Relics from Sinkiang Uighur Autonomous Region
(1st — 7th century A.D.)

247. Brocade mitten with the characters: Yen Nien Yi Shou
1st - 2nd century A.D. (Eastern Han)
Length 24 cm.
Unearthed in 1959 from a site at Niya, Minfeng county in Sinkiang

248, 249. Two pieces of woolen fabric with grape pattern
1st - 2nd century A.D. (Eastern Han)
Length 22.5 cm. and 26 cm.
Unearthed in 1959 from site at Niya, Minfeng county in Sinkiang

247

248, 249

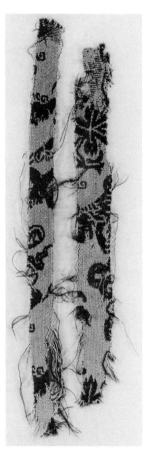

250

251

250. Woolen girdle
1st - 2nd century A.D. (Eastern Han)
Length 29 cm.
Unearthed in 1959 from a site at Niya, Minfeng
county in Sinkiang

251. Yellow damask with lozenge pattern
1st - 2nd century A.D. (Eastern Han)
Length 24.5 cm.
Unearthed in 1959 from a site at Niya, Minfeng
county in Sinkiang

252

252. Brocade with tree pattern
6th century A.D. (Northern Dynasties)
Length 20.5 cm.
Unearthed in 1959 from Astana, Turfan county
in Sinkiang

253. Blue woolen fabric with pattern dyed by the
wax-resist technique (batik)
5th century A.D. (Northern dynasties)
Length 11 cm.
Unearthed in 1959 from Wuyulaike, Yutien
county in Sinkiang

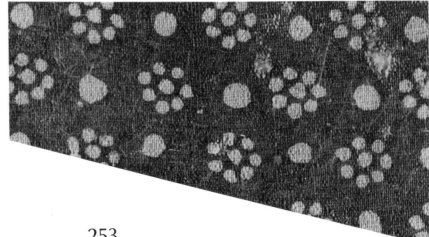

253

254

254. Brocade with flowers-and-birds design
8th century A.D. (Tang dynasty)
Length 38.2 cm.
Unearthed in 1968 from Astana, Turfan county
in Sinkiang

255. Brocade with motif of confronted birds
7th century A.D. (Tang dynasty)
Length 26 cm.
Unearthed in 1969 from Astana, Turfan county
in Sinkiang

255

256. Brocade with picture of a drinking pair
8th century A.D. (Tang dynasty)
Length 12.8 cm.
Unearthed in 1969 from Astana, Turfan county
in Sinkiang

257. Yellow gauze with design of confronted birds, dyed
by the wax-resist technique (batik)
8th century A.D. (Tang dynasty)
Length 57 cm.
Unearthed in 1968 from Astana, Turfan county
in Sinkiang

258. Tang dynasty register of household and land allocation:
household of Ning Ho-tsai, Kaochang County
689 A.D.
29 cm. x 82.3 cm.
Unearthed in 1964 from Astana, Turfan county in Sinkiang

259

260

261, 262

263

259. Loan contract signed by Pai Huai-lo as debtor
670 A.D.
29 cm. x 43 cm.
Unearthed in 1964 from Astana, Turfan county in Sinkiang

260. Fried bread-roll
7th century A.D. (Tang dynasty)
Length 18 cm.
Unearthed in 1960 from Astana, Turfan county in Sinkiang

261, 262. Two *chiaotzu* (dumplings)
7th century A.D. (Tang dynasty)
Length 5 cm. and 6 cm.
Unearthed in 1960 from Astana, Turfan county in Sinkiang

263. Silver Sassanian coin
Diameter 2.9 cm.
Unearthed in 1967 from Astana, Turfan county in Sinkiang

SUI DYNASTY
(581 — 618 A.D.)

XXV / Chang Sheng's Tomb of the Sui Dynasty at Anyang, Honan Province
(595 A.D.)

264. White porcelain figure of a warrior
Height 64 cm.

265 - 272. Eight painted pottery musicians
Height 17.2 cm. - 19 cm.

273. White porcelain figure of an
attendant, partly in black glaze
Height 71 cm.

273

XXVI / Surveys and Excavations of the Tang Capital Changan at Sian, Shensi Province, Discovered in 1970

274. Octagonal gold cup decorated with human figures
Height 5.4 cm., major axis 7 cm., minor axis 6.3 cm.

275. Silver box with bird and flower design
Height 6 cm., dia. 13.5 cm.

274

275

276. Silver bowl with gilt floral design
Height 3 cm., dia. of mouth 10.1 cm.

277. Silver winged-cup with gilt floral design
Height 2.8 cm., major axis 10.5 cm.,
minor axis 8.6 cm.

276

277

278

278. Covered silver bowl with gilt
    floral design
    Height 11.4 cm., dia. of
    mouth 21.9 cm.

279. Silver *yi* with gilt floral design
    Height 8.3 cm.

279

280

280. Gold bowl with embossed lotus-petal design
Height 5.5 cm., dia. of mouth 13.5 cm.

281 - 284. Silver box containing cinnabar and jade
     girdle ornaments
     Height of box 6.2 cm., dia. of mouth 17 cm.

285, 286. Silver box containing stalactite
     Height of box 6.4 cm., dia. of mouth 17 cm.

281 — 284

285, 286

287, 288

289, 290

291, 292

287, 288. Silver plate and cinnabar
Height of plate 1.9 cm., dia. of
mouth 14.4 cm.

289, 290. Amber and silver plate
Height of plate 1.9 cm., dia. of
mouth 14.3 cm.

291, 292. Rock crystal and silver plate
Height of plate 1.7 cm., dia. of
mouth 18.1 cm.

293, 294

293, 294. Amethyst and silver plate
Height of plate 1.7 cm., dia. of mouth
18.7 cm.

295. Silver vessel in shape of pomegranate
Height 8.9 cm.

295

297

296. Three-colored pottery horse
Height 28 cm.

297. Yellow-glazed pottery horse
Height 20.1 cm.

298. Three-colored pottery mounted hunter
Height 32 cm.

296

298

299

300

299. Three-colored pottery mounted hunter
     Height 31 cm.

300. Painted pottery horseman
     Height 32 cm.

301. Painted pottery horseman
     Height 30.5 cm.

302. Painted pottery
mounted hunter
Height 31.5 cm.

302

303. Three-colored pottery bowl
Height 7.4 cm., dia. of mouth
17.2 cm.

304. Three-colored pottery dish
Height 2.7 cm., dia. of mouth
15 cm.

305. Green-glazed pottery bowl
Height 8 cm., dia. of mouth
13.7 cm.

303

304

305

306. Women attendants, wall painting in the
tomb of Princess Yung Tai (copy)
192 cm. x 440 cm.

307, 308. Incised figures of palace ladies on the stone
     sarcophagus of Princess Yung Tai (rubbings)
     136 cm. x 81 cm.

307

308

XXVIII / Fine and Applied Arts of Tang Dynasty
(618 — 907 A.D.)

309. Three-colored pottery horse
    Early 8th century A.D.
    Height 80 cm., length 82.5 cm.
    Unearthed in 1971 from the tomb of Crown Prince Yi Teh
    at Chienhsien, Shensi

310, 311. Three-colored pottery pack-camel and groom
    8th century A.D.
    Height of groom 29.7 cm., height of camel 47.5 cm.,
    length 40 cm.
    Unearthed in 1959 at Chungpao village, Sian, Shensi

310, 311

312, 313

312, 313. Three-colored pottery horse and groom
8th century A.D.
Height of groom 29 cm., height of horse 40.6 cm.,
length 42.4 cm.
Unearthed in 1959 at Chungpao village, Sian, Shensi

312

314, 315. Three-colored pottery
figurines of women
8th century A.D.
Height 42 cm. and 45 cm.
Unearthed in 1959 at Chungpao
village, Sian, Shensi

314

315

316. Three-colored pottery warrior
     8th century A.D.
     Height 65.5 cm.
     Unearthed in 1959 at
     Chungpao village, Sian, Shensi

317. Three-colored pottery tomb-
     guardian
     8th century A.D.
     Height 57.5 cm.
     Unearthed in 1959 at
     Chungpao village, Sian, Shensi

317

318. Yellow-glazed pottery ox in lying position
8th century A.D.
Length 46 cm.
Unearthed in 1965 at Chinan county, Kansu

319. Three-colored phoenix-head vase
8th century A.D.
Height 32.2 cm.
Unearthed in 1961 at Loyang, Honan

318

320

320. Covered pot of three-colored pottery
8th century A.D.
Height 21 cm.
Unearthed in 1958 at Loyang, Honan

321. White porcelain spittoon
9th century A.D.
Height 10.5 cm.
Unearthed in 1955 at Sian, Shensi

321

322

322. High-stemmed porcelain bowl
with applied floral decoration
7th century A.D.
Height 23 cm.
Unearthed in 1956 at Sian, Shensi

323. Celadon vase with applied design in dark brown
9th century A.D.
Height 22.5 cm.
Unearthed in 1958 at Changsha, Hunan

323

324

324. Bronze mirror with hunting design
7th century A.D.
Diameter 29 cm.
Unearthed in 1961 at Fukou, Honan

325

325. Bronze mirror with double-phoenix design
7th century A.D.
Diameter 23 cm.
Unearthed in 1952 at Hsienyang, Shensi

326

326. Bronze mirror with bird and animal design
7th century A.D.
Diameter 21.5 cm.
Unearthed in 1955 at Sian, Shensi

327

328

327, 328. Procession scene,
wall painting in the tomb of
Crown Prince Chang Huai
(2 copies)
Early 8th century A.D.
150 cm. x 240 cm.,
148 cm. x 204 cm.

XXIX / Five Dynasties Tomb at Linan, Chekiang Province, Excavated in 1969
(10th century A.D.)

330

329. Porcelain vase with cloud design, Yueh ware
Height 50.7 cm.

330. Bowl, Yueh ware
Height 9.5 cm., dia. of mouth 19.9 cm.

331. Two-eared covered jar, Yueh ware
     Height 19.6 cm.

332. Two-eared kettle-shaped vessel, Yueh ware
     Height 9.2 cm., dia. of mouth 17.6 cm

332

XXX / Sung Dynasty Porcelain
(960 — 1279 A.D.)

333

334

333. Bowl with lotus flower design, Ting ware
10th century A.D.
Height 7.3 cm., dia. of mouth 21.9 cm.
Unearthed in 1969 from the foundation of the
Chingchih Monastery pagoda, Tinghsien
county, Hopei province

334. Porcelain conch, Ting ware
10th century A.D.
Height 19.8 cm.
Unearthed in 1969 from the foundation of
the Chingchih Monastery pagoda, Tinghsien
county, Hopei province

335. Censer with five feet, Ting ware
10th century A.D.
Height 24.1 cm.
Unearthed in 1969 from the foundation of the
Chingchih Monastery pagoda, Tinghsien
county, Hopei province

336

336. Flower-shaped dish marked with the
character "kuan", Ting ware
10th century A.D.
Height 3 cm., dia. of mouth 12.8 cm.
Unearthed in 1969 from the foundation of
the Chingchih Monastery pagoda,
Tinghsien county, Hopei province

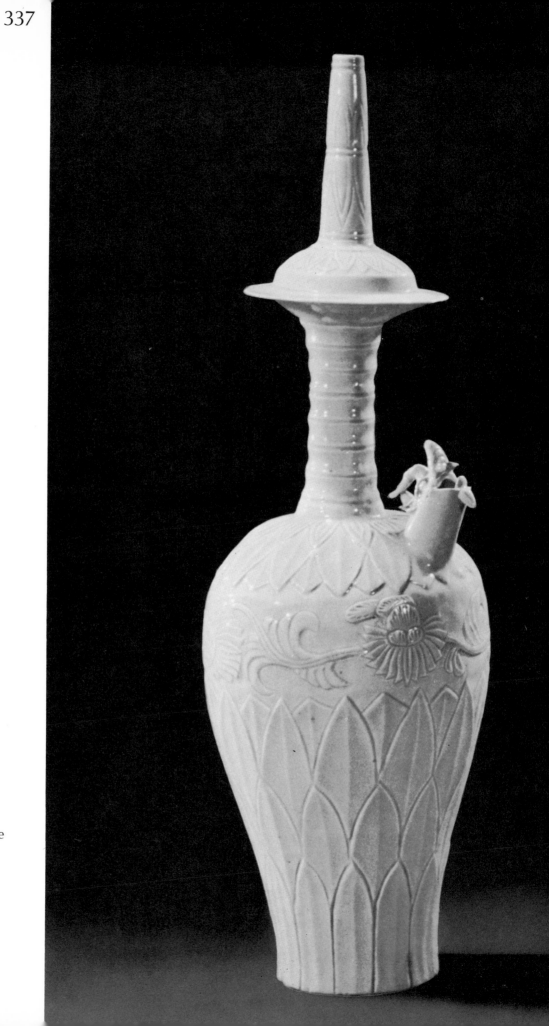

337. White vase *(kendi)* with
carved decoration, Ting ware
10th century A.D.
Height 60.5 cm.
Unearthed in 1969 from the
foundation of the
Chingchung Monastery
pagoda, Tinghsien county,
Hopei province

338

338. Flask incised with floral design, with a silver cover, Ting ware
     10th century A.D.
     Height 19.8 cm.
     Unearthed in 1969 from the foundation of the Chingchung
     Monastery pagoda, Tinghsien county, Hopei province

339. Vase decorated with dragon design, Lungchuan ware
12th century A.D.
Height 19 cm.
Unearthed in 1956 at the site of the Great Kiln *(Tayao)*,
Lungchuan county, Chekiang

340. Bowl with lotus-petal design, Lungchuan ware
    Early 13th century A.D.
    Height 6.5 cm., dia. of mouth 13.5 cm.
    Unearthed in 1960 at the site of the Great Kiln *(Tayao)*,
    Lungchuan county, Chekiang

341. Water-dropper in shape of a boat, Lungchuan ware
     12th century A.D.
     Length 17.3 cm.
     Unearthed in 1956 at Lungchuan, Chekiang

342

342. Tripod censer, Lungchuan ware
      Early 13th century A.D.
      Height 12.4 cm.
      Unearthed in 1954 at Juian county, Chekiang

343

343. Ying-ching wine pot with warmer
11th century A.D.
Height of pot 25.8 cm., height of warmer 14 cm.
Unearthed in 1963 at Susung, Anhwei

344

344. Ying-ching bowl
13th century A.D.
Height 9.8 cm.,
dia. 21.2 cm.
Unearthed in 1965 at
Tehan, Kiangsi

345

345. Ying-ching bowl incised
with floral design
12th century A.D.
Height 7.2 cm., dia. of
mouth 20.5 cm.
Unearthed in 1952 at
Nanchang, Kiangsi

346. Tripod censer, Yaochow ware
   13th century A.D.
   Height 27 cm.
   Unearthed in 1960 at Lantian, Shensi

346

347. Pillow with fishing design, Tzuchow ware
12th century A.D.
Length 28.8 cm.
Unearthed in 1955 at Hsingtai, Hopei

347

遼
金
元

XXXI / Tomb of a Liao Princess's Consort at Chihfeng, Liaoning Province, Excavated in 1953
(959 A.D.)

349

348. White porcelain plate marked with the character "kuan"
Height 5.4 cm., dia. of mouth 22.3 cm.

349. White porcelain flat flask ornamented with cockscomb
Height 23.5 cm.

348

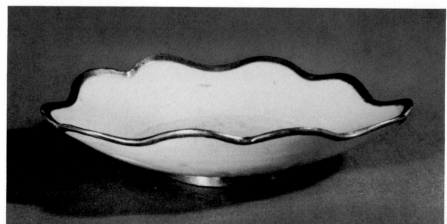

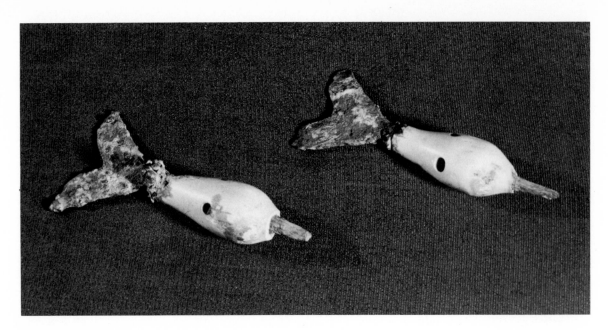

350, 351

350, 351. Two iron heads of
whistling arrows
Length 10 cm. and 9.5 cm.

352, 353. Two gilt silver saddle
ornaments
Height 27.7 cm. and 37.5 cm.

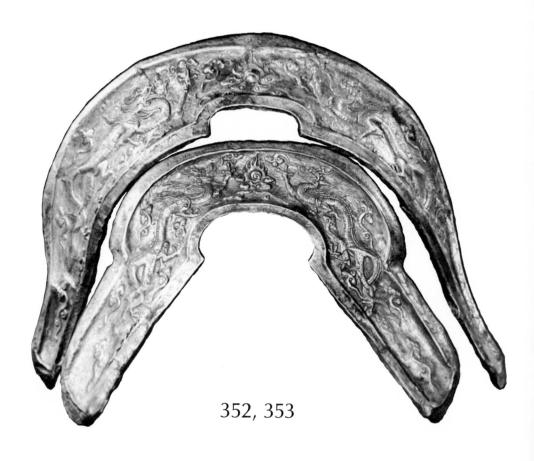

352, 353

354. Silver cup with stand
Height 8.5 cm., dia. of stand 16 cm.

355. Gilt silver tassel ornament for horse
Height 6 cm., dia. 19.2 cm.

354

355

XXXII / Pottery Dramatic Actors of the Kin and Yuan Dynasties
from Shansi and Honan Provinces
(1115 — 1368 A.D.)

356 — 358

356 - 358. Three pottery actors
13th century A.D. (Kin)
Height 19.5 cm. - 21 cm.
Unearthed in 1965 at Houma, Shansi

359

359. Pottery actor dancing
     14th century A.D. (Yuan)
     Height 39.2 cm.
     Unearthed in 1963 at Chiaotso, Honan

360

360. Pottery actor with clappers
14th century A.D. (Yuan)
Height 37 cm.
Unearthed in 1963 at Chiaotso, Honan

361

361. Pottery actor whistling
      14th century A.D. (Yuan)
      Height 37 cm.
      Unearthed in 1963 at Chiaotso, Honan

362

362. Ying-ching statuette
of Kuanyin
1st half of 14th
century A.D.
Height 66 cm.
Unearthed in 1955 in
west city of Peking

363

363. Openwork censer of three-colored glazed pottery
End of 13th century A.D.
Height 36 cm.
Unearthed in 1964 in the Haitien district of Peking

364

364. Covered jar with floral
     designs in underglaze red
     1st half of 14th century A.D.
     Height 66 cm.
     Unearthed in 1961 in the
     Haitien district of Peking

365. Blue-and-white porcelain vase
     1st half of 14th century A.D.
     Height 15.3 cm.
     Unearthed in 1962 in the
     west city of Peking

366

366. Plate, Chun ware
1st half of 14th century A.D.
Height 4.5 cm., dia. of mouth 22.3 cm.
Unearthed in 1969 at Fangshan, Peking

367. Ying-ching brush-rest
    1st half of 14th century A.D.
    Length 18 cm.
    Unearthed in 1962 in the west city of Peking

368. Porcelain jar decorated with two phoenixes in black on white ground
13th century A.D.
Height 36 cm.
Unearthed in 1970 at Fangshan, Peking

369. Blue-and-white covered pot decorated with
white dragon design
1st half of 14th century A.D.
Height 51.5 cm.
Unearthed in 1964 at Paoting, Hopei

370

370. Blue-and-white ewer with floral design
1st half of 14th century A.D.
Height 26.5 cm.
Unearthed in 1964 at Paoting, Hopei

371. Basin, Chun ware
13th century A.D.
Height 10.6 cm., dia. of mouth 44 cm.
Unearthed in 1955 at Paoting, Hopei

371

372. Silver confectionery box decorated with
    double-phoenix pattern
    1st half of 14th century A.D.
    15.9 cm., dia. 35 cm.
    Unearthed in 1955 at Hofei, Anhwei

373. Round box of lacquerware carved with human figures
1st half of 14th century A.D.
Height 3.9 cm., dia. 12.1 cm.
Unearthed in 1953 at Chingpu, Shanghai

373

374 — 385

374 - 385. Toilet articles and silver toilet box with stand (12 pieces)
    14th century A.D.
    Height of box 24.3 cm., dia. 17 cm., height of
    mirror-stand 30.4 cm.
    Unearthed in 1964 at Soochow, Kiangsu

NOTES

NOTES

THE CHINESE EXHIBITION
is an illustrated handlist of
The Exhibition of Archaeological Finds of the People's Republic of China
held at the
William Rockhill Nelson Gallery of Art
Atkins Museum of Fine Arts
from April twentieth through June eighth
nineteen hundred and seventy-five.

The design and typography of this volume are by
Richard A. Anderson
Composition in Optima by Pulliam-Marty Typographers, Inc.
Kansas City, Missouri
Produced by Burd & Fletcher, Kansas City, Missouri

Reprinted for the showing
of the exhibition at the

Asian Art Museum of San Francisco
The Avery Brundage Collection
San Francisco, California
from June twenty-eighth
through August twenty-eight
nineteen hundred and seventy-five.